The Armada Portrait

Christine Riding
Robert Blyth

First published in 2020 by the National Maritime Museum, Park Row, Greenwich, London SE10 9NF

www.rmg.co.uk

ISBN: 978-1-906367-68-8

At the heart of the UNESCO World Heritage Site of Maritime Greenwich are the four world-class attractions of Royal Museums Greenwich – the National Maritime Museum, the Royal Observatory, the Queen's House and *Cutty Sark*.

A CIP catalogue record for the book is available from the British Library.

Book design and typesetting by Thomas Bohm, User Design, Illustration and Typesetting

Cover design by Ocky Murray

Printed and bound in the UK on FSC certified paper by Gomer Press

Contents

Introduction: Elizabeth before the Armada

There are three known contemporary Armada portraits of Elizabeth I: the Woburn version in the collection of the Duke of Bedford at Woburn Abbey; the Greenwich version at the Queen's House, formerly owned by the Tyrwhitt-Drake family; and a third, somewhat cut-down version at the National Portrait Gallery in London. Each commemorates the most famous conflict of Elizabeth's long reign (1558–1603), the defeat of the Spanish Armada in 1588. This event was central to the Elizabethan age and cemented Elizabeth's reputation as a powerful and successful monarch. It is, therefore, of little surprise that her triumph was celebrated in a portrait that has become perhaps the most immediately recognisable depiction of the queen and, arguably, of any British monarch.

▲ The Armada Portrait at the Queen's House, Greenwich
16th-century English School, *c.* 1588, oil on panel, 1125 mm × 1270 mm

▲ The Armada Portrait at Woburn Abbey, Bedfordshire
George Gower, *c.*1588, oil on panel, 1235 mm × 1510 mm

▲ The Armada Portrait at the National Portrait Gallery, London
Unknown English artist, *c.* 1588, oil on panel, 978 mm × 724 mm

Elizabeth's path to the throne, however, was neither straightforward nor dynastically predestined. The fixation of her father, Henry VIII, on securing a male heir turned many of the certainties of Tudor England on their head. Henry and his first wife, Catherine of Aragon, had two children: Henry, Duke of Cornwall (b. 1511), who died in infancy; and Mary (b. 1516), who would eventually accede to the throne. Another son, the illegitimate Henry FitzRoy, was born to his mistress Elizabeth Blount in 1519. With little prospect of producing a legitimate male heir, Henry set about divorcing Catherine, a move that ultimately caused the English Reformation and the break with the Roman Catholic Church. Henry secretly wed Anne Boleyn on 14 November 1532 and his marriage to Catherine was formally annulled the following May, prompting the Pope to excommunicate the king. Princess Elizabeth was born at Greenwich Palace on 7 September 1533. The following year Anne fell pregnant again but had a miscarriage and Henry felt her failure to produce a son was a betrayal. In January 1536, Catherine of Aragon died, an event Henry and Anne regarded with joy, especially given that Anne was pregnant once again. However, at the end of the month she suffered another miscarriage, a son. At this stage the king was already pursuing Jane Seymour and Henry needed a way to end his second marriage. Correspondingly, Anne's enemies at court now conspired against her. They succeeded with fictitious allegations of adultery and high treason and, at Henry's command, she was executed at Tower Green in London on 19 May. Wasting no time, he married Jane Seymour

▲ *Henry VIII (1491–1547)*
   Studio of Hans Holbein, 16th century, oil on panel

the next day. Elizabeth was not yet two and now technically illegitimate like her half-sister Mary.

Jane Seymour delivered a healthy baby boy on 12 October 1537 following a difficult labour. The four-year-old Princess Elizabeth was present at the baptism of the infant, named Edward. But Queen Jane died twelve days later, having succumbed to septicaemia. With the male line now established,

▲ *Thomas Seymour, 1st Baron Seymour of Sudeley, c.1509–49*
Nicholas Denizot, *c.*1545–1549, oil on panel

Mary and Elizabeth were returned to 'legitimacy' by the Act of
Succession (1543): the princesses were now valuable diplomatic
commodities in the European royal marriage market.
Accordingly, Elizabeth received a well-rounded education
by the standards of the day, mastering languages (ancient and
modern), the classics and calligraphy. It was this serious and
scholarly girl that was painted by an unknown artist, possibly

William Scrots, in around 1546. Perhaps originally intended for Henry VIII, the portrait (part of the Royal Collection) was given to her half-brother. It shows a thoughtful Elizabeth, richly dressed in red and gold, gazing towards the viewer, holding a book with another volume open on a table.

But events were soon to shape the life of the adolescent princess and lead her into genuine danger. Henry VIII died on 27 January 1547 and the young Edward VI assumed the throne, aged just nine. Elizabeth now made her home with the dowager queen, Henry's sixth wife, Katherine Parr. With unseemly haste, Katherine married Thomas Seymour, a prominent courtier and the lord high admiral. The 14-year-old Elizabeth was certainly attracted to the handsome Seymour, who was more than 20 years her senior, and he took more than a respectful interest in the young princess. Eventually, with her suspicions aroused, Katherine intervened and in May 1548 Elizabeth was sent to live with Sir Anthony Denny and his wife Joan in Hertfordshire. However, that September Katherine died following the birth of a daughter. Seymour resumed his pursuit of Elizabeth, but he posed more than a sexual threat to her: she was now in political peril. Seymour was jostling for favour at court and sought to undermine the position of his elder brother, Edward, Duke of Somerset, as Protector during the young king's minority. With rumours of a conspiracy to marry Elizabeth and to kidnap Edward VI, Seymour's rather clumsy plotting against the regime soon brought about his downfall. He was found guilty of treason and beheaded on 20 March 1549. As the allegations were investigated, even some of Elizabeth's servants were arrested, embroiling her in the deadly affair. The risk to Elizabeth was now clear and present; she was interviewed to establish the nature of her involvement, but maintained a steely composure and said nothing to undermine her royal dignity. On the verge of adulthood, Elizabeth had survived a brutal and bloody introduction to the cut-throat world of the Tudor court. But greater trials were still to come.

In 1553, with his health failing, Edward VI outlined his plans for the future of the monarchy in a document known as the 'Devise'. He removed both Mary and Elizabeth from the line of royal succession for fear that their marriage to a foreign ruler might alter the course of English laws and, more importantly in the case of the Catholic Mary, the Protestant settlement. Through a convoluted development, the 'Devise' settled the succession on Lady Jane Grey (the great-granddaughter of Henry VII, who was presumptively fourth in line to throne under the terms of Henry VIII's will), whose as yet unborn male heirs would rule. As soon as it was clear the king would not recover from his illness, John Dudley, the scheming Duke of Northumberland, speedily arranged the marriage of Lady Jane to his son, Guildford. On 6 July 1553, Edward VI died at Greenwich Palace aged only 15. The terms of the 'Devise' were enacted, but Lady Jane Grey's hold on power as the pawn of her powerful and controlling manipulators was famously brief – indeed, she has become known as the 'nine days queen'. Mary, the rightful heir under the 1543 Act, marshalled her forces and was proclaimed queen on 15 July, ending the

▲ *Edward VI (1537–1553)*
 After Hans Holbein, 16th century, oil on panel

attempt to usurp the throne. The 16-year-old Jane was
executed on 12 February the following year.

For Elizabeth, Mary securing the throne was hardly a
source of reassurance. Her half-sister was a devout Roman
Catholic, who fervently sought to undo the Reformation
of Henry and Edward and return England to the papist fold.
Elizabeth was now vulnerable within the violent religious
politics of the new regime, both as a practising Protestant

in her own right and as a potential rallying figure for the plotting of now-oppressed Protestant courtiers. Indeed, such an event took place very early in Mary's reign when, unwittingly, Elizabeth discovered that Sir Thomas Wyatt of Kent had rebelled in her name. Elizabeth's life now hung in the balance and she was imprisoned in the Tower of London on 18 March 1554. Again she had to defend herself when interrogated by members of the privy council, and again she showed her determination. The immediate danger passed and Elizabeth was placed under house arrest at Woodstock in Oxfordshire, leaving the dreaded Tower on 19 May. It was clear, however, that the threat most emphatically remained and Elizabeth might fall foul of events beyond her control or knowledge.

To secure a Catholic succession, Mary needed to marry. This was a major step for a female ruler and, in addition, Mary would have been only too well aware of the risks of pregnancy for a childless woman in her late thirties. She sought the advice of Charles V of Spain, who had long defended her interests. Naturally, Charles was keen to see England return to Catholicism and equally keen to advance the interests of Spain and the Habsburgs. In what was a purely dynastic match, he suggested his son, Prince Philip, as a suitable husband. This royal union was the subject of extremely complex negotiations. Nevertheless, Philip arrived at Southampton on 20 July 1554, accompanied by a fleet of 80 large ships and over a hundred smaller vessels: an armada in all but name. These ships were carrying a substantial military force destined for the Spanish Netherlands, but Philip's personal entourage numbered some 3,000 courtiers and servants. Mary married Philip, who was ten years her junior, at Winchester Cathedral on 25 July. By November Mary believed, wrongly, she was pregnant, but the following July, with no prospect of a birth, Philip gave up hope of an heir. He left for the Continent that August and did not return until March 1557, remaining in England for only a few months. Philip and Mary parted company for

▲ *Mary I of England (1516–1558) and Philip II of Spain (1527–1598)*
English School, probably after Lucas de Heere, 16th century, oil on canvas

the last time on 8 July, when he left to go to war. Once again, by November Mary was certain she was pregnant, but this too proved false. Her health, never robust, broke down during 1558, giving Elizabeth an opportunity to prepare for the throne. Disliking her half-sister's Protestantism and relative popularity, Mary waited until almost the last moment before she declared Elizabeth as her heir on 6 November. She died on 17 November, aged 42.

Having survived a period of extraordinary upheaval and personal danger, the 25-year-old Elizabeth was now Queen of England and Ireland. During her 45-year reign, she had to overcome many difficulties associated with her sex and her religion. Marriage and the need to produce an heir were almost constant matters of discussion for at least two decades; and Catholic plots remained an ever-present threat. Elizabeth was also lucky to survive smallpox in 1562. However, the greatest crisis she faced was the Spanish Armada of 1588. Ever since, its defeat has marked both the zenith and the defining moment of Elizabeth's reign. Likewise, the Armada Portrait, produced to celebrate England's deliverance from the threat of Spanish invasion, has become *the* image of Gloriana, the Virgin Queen. ❀

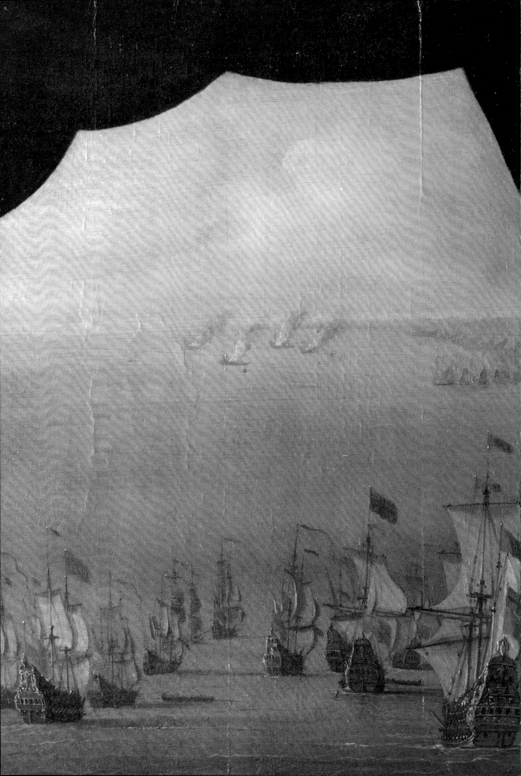

Elizabeth I and the Spanish Armada

The circumstances that led to England being under threat of invasion from Spain, the superpower of the day, were nothing short of a foreign relations catastrophe. If successful, the 1588 conquest of England would regain the English Crown for Philip II of Spain – which he had briefly held during his marriage to Elizabeth's half-sister Mary – and return the country to Roman Catholicism. It would not only end Elizabeth's reign but also leave western Europe dominated by Spain. The Henrician Reformation and break with Rome in the 1530s put England continually at odds with its Catholic neighbours. Furthermore, in 1570, when it became clear she would never be gathered into the Catholic fold, Elizabeth I was excommunicated by Pope Pius V. One important legacy of this ongoing tension was the incentive for sustained investment in the English navy with the express purpose of defending home waters. Spain's empire in the New World (otherwise known as the Spanish Main) was the source of enormous wealth and much coveted by England. From the 1560s, English sailors took to the high seas in increasing numbers and turned Protestant piracy into a global enterprise, plundering Spanish shipping in European and Atlantic waters. Francis Drake's repeated assaults upon Spain and its colonies included the looting and burning of over two dozen ships at Cadiz in April 1587. Largely through private enterprise, England also aspired to be an imperial power at this time. Unsuccessful attempts in 1584 and 1587 to establish the first English colony in the world, on the east coast of North America, resulted in Sir Walter Raleigh claiming the territory of 'Virginia' on behalf of Elizabeth, the Virgin Queen.

Another point of friction between Spain and England was Elizabeth's tacit support from the 1570s for the Protestant rebellions in the Spanish Netherlands and in France. In response, Philip II gave surreptitious aid to Catholic conspiracies against her throne and life. The timing was key. By the late 1580s, Elizabeth was in her mid-fifties, unmarried, childless and thus without an heir. Her Catholic cousin, Mary, Queen of Scots, had the best claim to the English throne, but in 1567 she had been forced to abdicate and flee to England, where she was imprisoned. In Scotland, her infant son became James VI. Over the succeeding years, the Scottish queen was at the centre of numerous plots against Elizabeth, so much so that many in England regarded Mary's continued existence as the greatest challenge to the Tudor regime and to the Protestant settlement. After much prevarication, being reluctant to behead a fellow monarch regardless of the cause, Elizabeth signed the death warrant at Greenwich on 1 February 1587. Mary's execution a week later made the Protestant James VI Elizabeth's heir. This was the final straw for Philip II and preparations to invade England were accelerated.

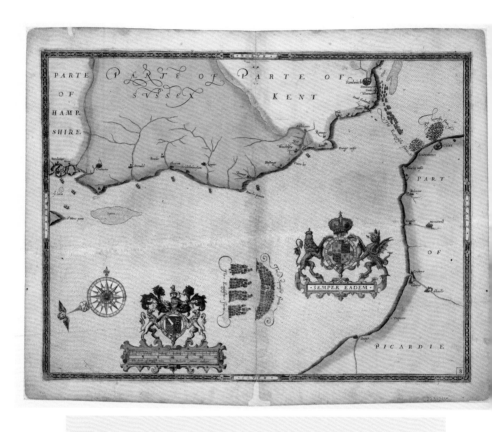

▲ The pursuit to Calais, 4–6 August 1588 from *Expeditionis Hispanorum in Angliam vera description Anno Do: MDLXXXVIII*
Augustine Ryther, after Robert Adams, 1590, printed and hand coloured

This printed chart is based on commander Lord Howard's official account of the Armada campaign. It shows the English fleet, in four squadrons, pursuing the Armada westwards in the Channel, and then the Armada at anchor off Calais, before the English attack on 7 August. The chart has Howard's coat of arms and those of the queen, with her motto *Semper Eadem*, 'Always the same'.

On 22 July 1588 the Spanish Armada, a force of roughly 130 ships and 18,000 men commanded by the 7th Duke of Medina Sidonia, left La Coruna in northern Spain and headed for the English Channel. Its rather complex objective was to rendezvous with a large army assembled in Flanders under the command of Alessandro Farnese, Prince of Parma and the governor of the Spanish Netherlands. These combined naval and military forces would then invade England. The naval balance of power between England and Spain in the summer of 1588 was delicately poised. The English fleet was comprised of royal ships and a large number of private vessels requisitioned from ports along the south coast and from as far north as Newcastle. Commanded by Lord Howard of Effingham, the lord high admiral, it outnumbered the Armada, but the Spanish ships were larger and more heavily armed. Much depended, therefore, on tactics, nerve and, as it turned out, luck. As the Armada was sighted off the English coast, beacons were lit, swiftly informing London and Elizabeth's court of its impending arrival. Skirmishes followed as the Armada neared Calais. The English then employed fireships to break up the Spanish fleet at its anchorage off Calais before engaging the Armada at the Battle of Gravelines on 8 August. Here superior English tactics proved crucial as did a change in the wind direction. The Armada was thus prevented from joining with Parma's forces and pursued into the North Sea, foiling the invasion.

While these dramatic events at sea were beyond Elizabeth's control, the unfolding crisis demanded resolute action by the queen ashore. Despite genuine fears of an assassination attempt,

➤ *Charles Howard,*
1536–1624, 1st Earl
of Nottingham
Daniel Mytens,
the Elder, about 1620,
oil on canvas

Charles Howard, the
lord high admiral, was in
overall command of the
English fleet that engaged
the Armada. He relied
on a council of war –
a meeting of his senior
commanders, including
experienced officers like
Francis Drake and John
Hawkins – to determine
the broad tactics to be
employed. Once a battle
began, Howard had few
means of controlling the
tactical deployment of
his squadrons as there
was essentially no system
of signalling. Therefore,
adhering to the consensus
of the council decision,
relying on the ability of
individual commanders
and hoping for a substantial
degree of luck were key
elements of the response
to the Armada.

she decided to make a personal appearance at Tilbury on the Thames Estuary, where English forces of around 17,000 men were deployed to repulse any Spanish landing. On 9 August, after inspecting the troops on horseback, she delivered the most famous speech of her reign:

'My loving people, we have been persuaded by some that are careful of our safety to take heed how we commit ourself to armed multitudes for fear of treachery; but I assure you, I do not desire to live to distrust my faithful and loving people.

Let tyrants fear. I have always so behaved myself that, under God, I have placed my chiefest strength and safe guard in the loyal hearts and good will of my subjects, and therefore I am come amongst you, as you see, at this time, not for my recreation and disport, but being resolved, in the midst and heat of the battle, to live or die amongst you all, to lay down my life for my God and for my kingdom and for my people, my honour, and my blood, even in the dust.

I know I have the body of a weak and feeble woman, but I have the heart and stomach of a king, and a king of England too, and think foul scorn that Parma or Spain, or any prince of Europe should dare to invade the borders of my realm; the which, rather than any dishonour shall grow by me, I myself will take up arms, I myself will be your general, judge, and rewarder of every one of your virtues in the field.'

▲ *Launch of fireships against the Spanish Armada, 7 August 1588*
  16th–century Netherlandish school, about 1590, oil on canvas

On 7 August, the Armada was closely anchored off Calais. At this point the English employed fireships, vessels containing combustible materials that were set ablaze and allowed to drift towards the Spanish fleet. This proved highly effective. While the Spanish did not panic, the fireships drove them from their anchorage and, as the weather conditions worsened, it became clear the Armada would be unable to return to Calais. The opportunity to combine with Parma's land forces was lost.

The purpose of the visit and speech was to galvanise English determination ahead of a potential confrontation with the Spanish army. It was far from clear how the largely untested English forces would react when faced by the Duke of Parma's men, or what competencies would be demonstrated by the queen's commanders. But despite these concerns, in reality the danger had already passed. Harried by the English in the North Sea, the Armada attempted to sail around Scotland and down the west coast of Ireland, and then return to Spain. However, terrible Atlantic storms, and shortages of food and water, battered the ships and ravaged their crews.

With victory, Elizabeth's status as a European monarch was immeasurably enhanced. For many within the British Isles and on the Continent, the Queen of England was now the defender of Protestant Europe. Poems, pamphlets and engravings extolled Elizabeth as the vanquisher of the Catholic threat. Medals struck to celebrate the Armada's defeat proclaimed it a Protestant victory; the storms that lashed and scattered the enemy fleet were evidence of divine intervention on behalf of Elizabeth's cause. That the mighty Armada failed to subdue a relatively small, island nation, made clear to other foreign powers that the Spanish were not as invincible as they would have the world believe. Consequently, England with its female ruler could not be dismissed as marginal in matters of commerce and diplomacy. This was particularly the case with Muslim powers that were fighting Catholic Spain in the Mediterranean. For example, Elizabeth was known as 'sultana Isabel' at the Moroccan court, an indication of her widespread prestige. In fact, before and more especially after 1588,

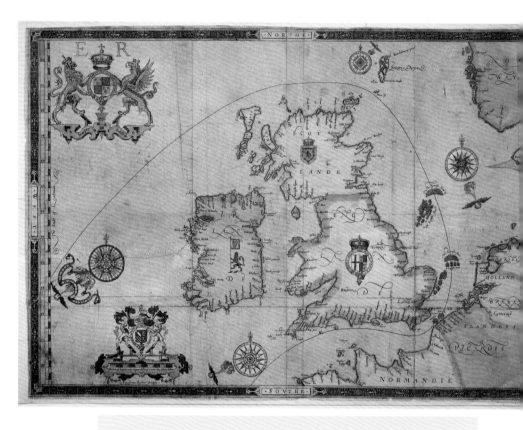

▲ The track of the Armada around Britain and Ireland from *Expeditionis Hispanorum in Angliam vera description Anno Do: MDLXXXVIII* Augustine Ryther, after Robert Adams, 1590, printed and hand coloured

This track chart shows the progress of the Armada; first through the Channel, culminating in the encounters at Calais and Gravelines, then the harrying pursuit by the English up the east coast and, finally, the Armada's dispersal in the face of Atlantic storms during the chaotic and costly return to Spain. Various Spanish vessels are shown wrecked along the Scottish and, more especially, Irish coasts.

▲ Medal commemorating the defeat of the Spanish Armada
  Unknown maker, Netherlands, 1588, silver

The defeat of the Armada was widely celebrated in the Protestant
Netherlands. This commemorative medal was struck soon after and is a
brazen piece of anti-Spanish and anti-Catholic propaganda. The obverse
shows a Catholic council of kings and bishops presided over by the Pope.
They have bandaged eyes and their feet are impaled on spiked floor. The
Latin mottos read: 'Oh! the blind minds, the blind hearts of men' and 'It is
hard to kick against the pricks'. On the reverse, Spanish ships are dashed
against a rock with seamen thrown into the waves. This emphatic image of
defeat is surrounded by a Latin inscription: 'Thou God art great and doest
wondrous things; thou art God alone'.

there was an extraordinary alignment between England
and the Islamic world – cultural, political and economic –
of a depth that arguably would not be experienced again
until the modern age. ❁

⋀ Medal commemorating the defeat of the Spanish Armada
Gerard van Bylaer, Netherlands, 1588, silver

Prince Maurice of Orange (1567–1625) led the Dutch revolt against Spain
in the Netherlands and he commissioned this medal to mark the defeat of
the Armada. The iconography of the obverse makes clear the Protestant
belief of divine intervention on behalf of their cause. It shows English and
Spanish ships engaged in battle; above, a stylised cloud, within which is
inscribed 'Jehovah' in Hebrew, issues forth gusts of wind. The surrounding
Latin motto reads: 'He blew and they were scattered'.

The Armada Portrait

The significance of the Armada Portrait

First and foremost, the Armada Portrait takes its place among the patriotic and eulogistic outpourings of post-1588 England. It also suggests the way in which the victorious queen and her kingdom might transform the balance of power within Europe, around the Mediterranean and even in the Americas. However, the portrait is in many ways a glorious fiction, disguising a complex and altogether less radiant reality. The Armada may have been defeated but it was hardly destroyed: over two-thirds of its ships returned to Spain. In 1589, the English launched the disastrous Counter Armada, commanded jointly by Sir Francis Drake and Sir John Norris, and there were further Spanish and English Armadas in the 1590s, all unsuccessful. With his armed forces engaged on a number of different fronts, Philip II's decision to embark on 'the enterprise of England' in 1588 can be described as a supreme case of imperial overreach. Even so, in terms of long-term damage to Spanish interests, the outcome had relatively little effect. But fighting with Spain intermittently over some two decades, the undeclared Anglo-Spanish War, put a terrible financial strain on the Elizabethan state. Elizabeth's successor, James VI (who became

James I of England and Ireland), lost little time in bringing hostilities to an end with the Treaty of London of 1604. Despite the imperial claims made within the Armada Portrait (and elsewhere), at Elizabeth's death in 1603, England had yet to establish an empire anywhere outside of the British Isles.

In this regard, the Armada Portrait does not represent what Elizabeth, her advisers and her courtiers thought was the case in 1588. Rather, given continuing anxieties and uncertainties at home and abroad, it was an image of what they wanted people to believe and to aspire to. Importantly, the painting could be said to encapsulate a fundamental shift in the English psyche that revealed itself during the Anglo-Spanish War. No longer would-be European conquerors in the mould of Henry V on the battlefields of France, the Elizabethans increasingly identified themselves as an island people, looking outward to the wider world beyond their shores. Although often threatened from abroad, they were (as the 1588 Armada had proved) capable not only of punching above their weight, but also of becoming a formidable global power in their own right. Like other portraits of Elizabeth I dating from the 1580s to her death in 1603, therefore, the Armada Portrait is a multilayered representation that forms part of the cult of Elizabeth, as the 'Empresse of the world', the 'Virgin Queen' and the embodiment of her island realm. While such portraits were calculated to flatter, they also underscore Elizabeth's appreciation of the power of images in the construction and exercise of might and authority. More particularly, they held the potential to help overcome

▲ *The Somerset House conference, 19 August 1604*
   After Juan Pantoja de la Cruz, *c.* 1604, oil on canvas

This very large group portrait commemorates the treaty of peace between
England and Spain in 1604. When James I ascended the throne in 1603
he was determined to end the 20-year war with Spain. This coincided with
Philip III of Spain's realisation that there was little chance of achieving his
father's aim of the destruction of Protestantism in England, and so he too
was anxious to end hostilities. The peace negotiations between England and
Spain, took place at Somerset House on the Strand, London, from May to
August 1604.

the cultural prejudices against her sex and to advertise her virtues, skills and competence as a (female) head of state.

With its complex use of symbols and metaphor, the Armada Portrait eloquently visualises Elizabeth's self-presentation as a learned queen. This was further demonstrated by the emphasis she placed on her linguistic skills and virtuoso performances when delivering speeches or engaging in debates, whether before the court, foreign embassies, parliament or the universities. (It is worth remembering here that portraits of Elizabeth were gifted, commissioned and displayed by these bodies.) Indeed, her skilful play on *female* vulnerability and strength in the Tilbury speech, delivered before a *male* audience, is the most memorable aspect of this now celebrated event. One detail of significance here is that Elizabeth's sumptuous dress (as suggested by the costume historian Janet Arnold) may have been that worn by the queen at Tilbury, a tantalising possibility that neatly underlines the powerful interrelationship between the speech and the portrait, between word and image.

Elizabeth's apparently impressive military record against the forces of despotism and popery, affirmed through such imagery as the Armada Portrait, became the standard by which her Stuart successors, and their policies, were judged by the public. Indeed, as the historian David Scott has noted, Elizabeth's carefully crafted but fictitious image as a Protestant heroine made her an almost impossible act to follow. Thus, as the popularity of the Stuarts waned during the seventeenth century, the myth of 'Good Queen Bess', 'Gloriana' and the Elizabethan 'Golden Age' took hold. Her female successors, Queen Anne and Queen Victoria, drew on her reputation,

The writing at the bottom of the engraving reads:

'T.h admired Empresse through the worlde applauded, Unto the eares of every forraigne Nation,
For supreme Virtues rares t. Imitation : Cannopey'd under powreful Angells wings
Whose Scepters rule fames lowde-voyc'd trumpet lawdeth, To her Immortall praise sweete Science sings
Are to be sould in Pauls head Alley by Io Sudbury and Geor Humble.

▲ *Queen Elizabeth I 1533–1603*
 Isaac Oliver, William Rogers, *c.*1600, engraving

The writing at the bottom reads: 'The admired Empresse through the
worlde applauded unto the eares of every forraigne Nation, for supreme
virtues rarest imitation. Connopey'd under powreful Angells wings whole
scepters rule fames lowde-voyc'd trumpet lawdets, to her immortall praise
sweete science sings.'

image and memory – as an authoritative woman in a predominantly male world – in the representation of their own rule. Indeed, a succession of monarchs and politicians, from William III to Winston Churchill, invoked her words to rally the nation. In addition, the idea began to establish itself that the triumph of 1588 marked the moment of Britain's inexorable rise to naval and imperial greatness. The Armada also became synonymous with the dark menace of invasion and despotism, and victory came to signal a bright future of English/British liberty and ascendancy. This patriotic trope was used time and again at moments of national crisis, particularly when Britain stood against Revolutionary and Napoleonic France, and later Nazi Germany. ❀

Making and comparing the Armada Portraits

Given the significance of the defeat of the Armada for Elizabeth and her kingdom, it is not surprising that there were at least three early versions of the Armada Portrait and in addition a number of surviving later copies and derivations. The Greenwich version is an oil painting on oak panels measuring 1125 × 1270 mm and is displayed in a later English eighteenth-century carved giltwood frame. The queen is shown three-quarter length, in a rich gold-embroidered and jewelled dress, as the epitome of royal magnificence. Her right hand rests on a terrestrial globe showing the Americas, which sits on a table, and she holds a fan made of ostrich feathers in her left hand. Beside her, and symbolically above the globe, an imperial 'covered' crown can be seen on a second table and, on the other side, a richly upholstered throne or chair of state. The two seascapes in the background, framed by dark green drapes, show (left) the English fleet in calm waters preparing to engage as, in the distance, English fireships head towards the Armada and (right) Spanish ships wrecked on the Irish coast in a menacing storm. These scenes are later versions, probably painted shortly after 1710 by a Dutch-trained artist working in England. Broadly speaking, they follow, in a later style with contemporary ships, the sixteenth-century subject matter underneath. The original appearance of these seascapes can be judged by those in the version of the Armada Portrait at Woburn Abbey. In addition, the collection at the National Maritime Museum contains a comparable Armada marine painting dating from the 1590s showing the two fleets in combat, probably at the Battle of Gravelines.

The Armada Portrait in the collection of the Duke of Bedford, which is documented at Woburn Abbey by 1782, was long thought to be by George Gower, but this attribution has recently been questioned. A third version in the National Portrait Gallery, which has also been attributed to Gower, once belonged to the Scottish peer and antiquarian David Steuart Erskine, the 11th Earl of Buchan (1742–1829). He presented it to the British Museum in 1765 and it was subsequently transferred to the National Portrait Gallery in 1879. This portrait is rather truncated (978 × 724 mm) having been cut down on both sides and possibly the lower edge. The Woburn version measures 1235 × 1510 mm and is thus a slightly different shape to the Greenwich version, and the composition stops more abruptly at the lower edge, cropping out some of the queen's left hand and perhaps also the queen's fan. It is accepted that the Greenwich version is by a different hand to the other two, given its distinctive techniques and approaches to the modelling of the queen's features. Moreover, it is thought that the three versions are the output of different workshops under the direction of unknown English artists. This would explain the variations in style, palette and details between the works.

▲ *English Ships and the Spanish Armada, August 1588*
English school, 16th century, oil on panel

This depiction of an Anglo-Spanish engagement may represent the Battle of Gravelines, 8 August 1588, but seems to be a commentary on the Armada campaign as a whole. With its flattened perspective, it is tempting to think it was produced as a tapestry design. While it conveys the scale and drama of the Armada, this is no straightforward battle scene: the painting contains subtly concealed elements of anti-Catholic satire. On board the central Spanish galleass, which flies a papal banner, is a jester surrounded by figures, including sinister religious zealots led by a preaching monk. The vessel has become a 'ship of fools', metaphorically embodying Catholic tyranny. While in a boat astern, emphasising the frustration of Spanish ambition, is a distraught Spaniard, perhaps Philip II or the commander, Medina Sidonia.

Who painted the Armada Portrait at Greenwich remains a matter of conjecture, but current scholarship suggests they were English. As such, it is certainly one of the earliest examples of a large-scale work in oils by any English artist, at a time when many artists working at the Tudor court were from the Continent. Historically, the portrait has been connected to the two most important English-born artists of the age: George Gower (d. 1596), who became Sergeant Painter to the Queen from 1581; and Nicholas Hilliard (c. 1547–1619), who was the queen's limner (miniaturist) and goldsmith from about 1573, and responsible for some of the most famous images of Elizabeth I. Another question surrounding the Armada Portrait at Greenwich is who commissioned or owned it. The person most often mentioned in this regard is Sir Francis Drake. One of the great heroes of Elizabeth's court, Drake was a sea captain, circumnavigator and pirate, whose exploits have achieved almost legendary status. Credited with the European discovery of San Francisco Bay, he was certainly the first English official to set foot on the Pacific coast of the New World. Knighted by Elizabeth I in 1581, Drake (and others) enriched the royal treasury and himself by plundering Spanish ships, actions that, in part, provoked the crisis of 1588. Importantly, he was vice-admiral in command of the English fleet against the Armada. As a courtier, patriot, proto-imperialist and a commander of the English fleet in 1588, it is difficult to imagine a painting of greater relevance to Drake than the Armada Portrait. Intriguingly, the portrait is securely documented at the home of one branch of Drake's heirs, Shardeloes in Buckinghamshire, with frequent references in print sources, starting in 1801;

manuscript references from the eighteenth century also exist, placing it in the house a generation earlier. The painting has passed down through the Tyrwhitt-Drake family, via the descendants of Drake's second wife, Elizabeth Sydenham.

While the authorship and early ownership of the Armada Portrait at Greenwich are open to question, the development of the painting itself is more firmly established. During Elizabeth's reign there were a number of attempts to regulate the quality and nature of images of the queen. Art historians have noted a series of face patterns deployed in her portraits. These follow a basic pattern for the representation of Elizabeth's face. They allowed the artist to paint the queen in an 'approved' manner, while granting a modest degree of freedom with regard to clothing, the inclusion of objects loaded with meaning (known as 'attributes') and the nature of the setting. The first of these was the 'Darnley' pattern that survives in numerous portraits. It was named after a portrait of about 1575 in the National Portrait Gallery's collection, which was acquired from the Earls of Darnley. Leaving aside

➤ *Elizabeth I, 1533–1603*
16th-century English school, *c.* 1590, oil on panel

This portrait is one of a number of 'workshop' paintings based on the 'Darnley' pattern. The artist is unknown, although the portrait has been linked to John Bettes, the Younger (*fl.* 1570–*d.* 1615). The queen is shown seated on a chair of state, richly attired in a bejewelled dress of black and white, holding a sceptre; in other portraits of this type she holds elaborate fans. The green and gold background is probably meant to represent tooled and gilded leather, adding to the courtly magnificence of the image.

▲ *Elizabeth I*
  Nicholas Hilliard, *c.*1585, pen and ink on vellum

Hilliard produced this full-length portrait of Elizabeth as one of a number of variant designs for the new Great Seal of 1584–86. A new seal was a major royal commission and the queen wanted to see several options before reaching a decision. It is possible that Hilliard's officially sanctioned 'pattern' formed the basis of that for the Armada Portrait.

the authorship of the oil paintings, the origin of the 'Armada' pattern undoubtedly lies with Hilliard, who was responsible for a number of miniatures of the 1580s showing the queen's head and shoulders, similarly posed to the Armada Portrait, with comparable headdress, circular ruff with the same arrangements of bows and pearls. Hilliard's involvement in the design of the 'Armada' pattern is further suggested by a drawing in the Victoria and Albert Museum (V&A). Variously described as a portrait of Elizabeth I or an Elizabethan lady, the dress clearly resembles the one worn in the Armada Portrait. Given that the facial features are not those of Elizabeth, it has been suggested that this drawing shows a lady-in-waiting posing in the queen's clothes to reduce the necessity of a lengthy sitting by the monarch herself. This further suggests that the 'Armada' pattern, and thus the Armada Portraits, was an 'official' representation of Elizabeth, in so far as it had been created with the cooperation and approval of the queen. Portraits of Elizabeth were commissioned as official gifts to foreign monarchs and to show to her prospective suitors, and courtiers acquired paintings and miniatures, the latter worn at court, to demonstrate their devotion to her. Hence the studios of Tudor artists produced many images of Elizabeth working from approved 'patterns' to meet this growing demand, which would have been viewed at the time as a mark of loyalty and reverence for Elizabeth. On occasion, the queen would make a gift of her portrait to a favoured member of the court. For example, she presented Drake with the celebrated locket known as the 'Drake Jewel', concealing a miniature portrait of her by Hilliard, one following the 'Armada' pattern, which Drake is shown wearing in the 1591 portrait in the National Maritime Museum's collection. The 'Drake Jewel', currently on loan to the V&A, still belongs to a different branch of Drake's descendants. The 'Armada' pattern has also been employed in a full-length format, examples being the portrait of Elizabeth I by an unknown artist at Trinity College, Cambridge, and another from the studio of Hilliard is on display at Hardwick Hall, the Elizabethan country house built for Bess of Hardwick. ⚘

➤ *Sir Francis Drake, 1540–96*
Marcus Gheeraerts, the Younger, 1591, oil on canvas

This portrait shows Drake following his successful role in the defeat of the Spanish Armada. The terrestrial globe on the table, turned to the broad expanse of the Atlantic, emphasises his great circumnavigation of 1577–80, during which he successfully plundered Spanish ships and ports. This not only netted a vast fortune for himself, but also provided sufficient loot to clear the national debt, earning Drake a knighthood and the gift of a jewel, which he wears on a long cord around his neck. Needless to say, Drake's actions did little to endear Elizabethan England to the Spanish.

The Armada Portrait and the image of Elizabeth I

Tudor portraits, no matter how simple and straightforward they may appear at first glance, invariably contain symbolic objects and references that carried meaning, whether private or public, to contemporary viewers. While this is true of the earliest portraits of Elizabeth, from the mid-1570s representations of her became more layered and nuanced, combining the symbols and attributes of monarchy, dynasty and empire with representations of chastity, purity and divinity, thus creating an entirely new iconography that promoted the majesty and significance of Elizabeth as the Virgin Queen.

➤ *Queen Elizabeth I, c.1580* [the Wanstead (or Peace) Portrait]
Marcus Gheeraerts, the Elder, *c.*1585, oil on panel

Here the queen is shown holding an olive branch, symbolising peace, with a sword of state, an emblem of justice, at her feet. Also included are a throne, covered in red cloth embroidered with gold and framed by the royal coat of arms. These are clear and unambiguous references to the idea of stability and good government that images of Elizabeth exude. The scene in the walled garden and figures to the right may allude to the house at Wanstead of her favourite, Robert Dudley, the Earl of Leicester.

The Armada Portrait

The Darnley Portrait of the mid-1570s features a crown and sceptre on a table beside the queen. This was the first appearance of these symbols of sovereignty separately used as props or attributes (rather than worn and carried) in Tudor portraiture, a theme that would be expanded in later portraits. For example, in the Peace Portrait (attributed to the Flemish Protestant master Marcus Gheeraerts the Elder and part of the Portland Collection at Welbeck Abbey, page 57), the sword of state, which is also a symbol of justice, lies at the queen's feet, alongside a dog representing fidelity, as she leans on a throne or chair of state, behind which the 'clothe of estate' bears her royal arms. Similarly, in the Ermine Portrait by Nicholas Hilliard (at Hatfield House), the sword lies on a table next to the queen. Above that can be seen a small, 'spotless' white ermine, with a gold crown as a collar, thus combining a symbol of purity with that of royal authority. In an earlier painting of 1572, *An Allegory of the Tudor Dynasty* (part of the Royal Collection), Elizabeth is shown entering the throne room to the right of her father, Henry VIII, accompanied by female figures representing

➤ *Queen Elizabeth I, 'The Ermine Portrait', 1585*
Unknown artist, 1585, oil on panel

The dazzling display of jewels in this portrait, showing Elizabeth as Pax with an olive branch, was probably drawn from life. Among the great strings of black pearls is the 'Three Brothers' pendant, once owned by the Dukes of Burgundy and bought by Henry VIII. It consists of three large rubies surrounding a substantial diamond. The pendant was later adapted and worn by James I as a hat jewel, before being pawned and lost to history.

Peace and Plenty. This is contrasted with the portraits of Mary I and Philip II of Spain on the left, which are accompanied by Mars, the Roman god of war. Dispensing with such allegorical figures, the later Peace and Ermine Portraits show Elizabeth holding an olive branch, thereby firmly establishing the queen herself as the bringer, or even the embodiment, of peace and stability. The juxtaposition of harmony and strife is represented in both the Armada Portrait and the Ditchley Portrait (see page 68) by the contrasting scenes of calm and storm that are positioned behind Elizabeth. Furthermore, in both paintings, the queen symbolically turns her back on the storm, her face turned towards tranquillity.

The backdrop to this significant shift in representing Elizabeth primarily concerns her gender and age. Since her accession to the throne in 1558, Elizabeth's marriage and her ability to produce an heir were matters of state and of international relations. In her twenties and thirties, there was still a strong possibility for both to happen (even Philip II had offered his hand in marriage after the death of Mary). But as the queen entered her forties and even more so her fifties, such hopes faded to nothing. It is also worth remembering that Elizabeth was only the second female monarch of England to reign in her own right. Furthermore, her enemies at home and abroad habitually focused on her illegitimacy, stemming both from her earlier removal from the royal line of succession by Henry VIII and from her Protestantism, which in turn 'legitimised' all attempts to remove her from the throne. The long-established trope of Elizabeth as the 'Protestant whore' was used as propaganda during the Armada crisis, for example, in a Catholic tract of July 1588 that accused the queen of sexual depravity with numerous members of her court, noting that 'she hath abused her body, against God's law, to the disgrace of princely majesty'. That her reputation was vulnerable in the face of such gendered taunts may well explain why the queen chose black and white as her personal colours, which (in Tudor colour symbolism) represent eternal virginity, white for chastity and black for constancy. This combination not only features in her dress worn in the Sieve (page 62), Ermine (page 59) and Armada Portraits, but was also worn by courtiers in deference to the queen.

In this context, the many symbols of purity in Elizabeth's portraits – such as ermine or pearls – are deployed not as mere flattery towards a queen, but rather to make the case that Elizabeth's legitimacy and competence as a monarch are intimately connected with her virgin state. This can be seen in the Sieve Portrait of 1583 by Quentin Massys the Younger at the Pinacoteca Nazionale in Siena. Dressed in black and white, the queen holds a sieve, a symbol of purity, and more specifically a reference to Tuccia, the Vestal Virgin, who (as relayed in Petrarch's *The Triumph of Chastity*) proved her virginity by carrying water in a sieve without spillage. The classical references continue with the pillar on the left of the portrait, which displays scenes from the story of Dido and Aeneas. In the final scene, Aeneas rejects Dido, Queen of Carthage, in order to fulfil his destiny as the founder of the Roman Empire. The message here seems to be that Elizabeth, in rejecting her suitors (perhaps represented by the courtiers milling on the right), has taken control of her passions to

◄ *Sieve Portrait of Queen Elizabeth I in Ceremonial Costume, c.1583*
Quentin Massys, the Younger, 1583, oil on canvas

This portrait shows the increasing symbolic sophistication surrounding the queen as her image developed over time. Now fifty, any hope of producing an heir had passed. The inclusion of the sieve, an emblem of chastity, now casts Elizabeth as the 'Virgin Queen'. However, on either side is evidence of the new focus of her reign: empire. The 'imperial' column and the globe suggest that overseas territory rather than dynasty will be Elizabeth's legacy to England.

focus on the good government of her kingdom. Furthermore, she will not only govern alone, with justice and righteousness, as head of state, but will also pursue her – and the state's – imperial ambitions. The inclusion of the globe on her left, turned to show the British Isles, represents the realm already in her unfaltering grasp and, with English ships shown sailing out into the Atlantic, perhaps the territories to come. These ideas were further developed in a print, based on the Sieve Portrait and published in the 1590s, which shows Elizabeth holding the royal regalia and standing between two classical columns. This motif was employed to celebrate Charles V's empire in the New World with the columns representing the Pillars of Hercules, the westernmost point of the Classical world, which his dominions far exceeded. The left column in the print is surmounted by the pelican devise, with chicks feeding upon blood from their mother's breast; the right is topped by the phoenix devise, perhaps an allusion to the perpetuity of monarchy. Both symbols were employed in

ELIZABETA D. G. ANGLIÆ. FRANCIÆ. HIBERNIÆ. ET VERGINIÆ
REGINA CHRISTIANAE FIDEI VNICVM PROPVGNACVLVM.

Immortalis honos Regum, cui non tulit ætas
 Ulla prior, veniens nec feret ulla parem,
Sospite quo nunquam terras habitare Britannas
 Desinet alma Quies, Iustitia atque Fides,

Queis ipsæ tantum superant reliqua omnia regna,
 Quantum tu maior Regibus es reliquis,
Viue precor felix tanti in moderamine regni,
 Dum tibi Rex Regum cælica regna paret.

In honorem serenissimæ suæ Maiestatis hanc effigiem fieri curabat Ioannes Woutnelius belga. Anno 1596.

earlier portraits of the queen by Nicholas Hilliard. Behind
Elizabeth, stretches her island realm, surrounded by the sea and
ships. The inscription beneath declares her Queen of England,
France (a reference to the much-lamented loss of England's
French possessions), Ireland *and* Virginia.

The Armada Portrait at Greenwich mirrors the imperial
symbolism in the Sieve Portrait (page 62), primarily through
the globe (the Woburn and National Portrait Gallery versions
also include classical columns), which is now turned to show
the Americas in a further allusion to the as yet unconquered
Virginia claimed beneath her outstretched hand. The imperial
crown on the table recalls the Darnley Portrait (page 49),
and the inclusion of the chair of state was previously employed
in the Peace Portrait. While the crown has often been
interpreted as signifying the pursuit of empire, with Elizabeth
cast as 'Empresse of the World', it also represents the claim made
by the Tudors that they were descended from Brutus of Troy,

who was by legend descended from Aeneas (as represented in the Sieve Portrait, page 62) and the mythical founder and first king of Britain. In this context, the Armada Portrait is an emphatic reassertion of Elizabeth's right to rule, not the Americas but the realm she inherited, which, through divine providence, she had now successfully defended. Hence the seascapes in the background of the portrait serve to represent two events from the Armada of 1588 and also visualise, using the classical 'ship of state' analogy, the effect of good Protestant governance under Elizabeth (the calm to the left), juxtaposed with the effect of tyrannical Catholic rule under Philip II (the chaotic storm to the right).

If the main theme of the Armada Portrait is the defence of the realm, then the portrayal of Elizabeth herself is telling. In her defiant speech at Tilbury, she proclaimed that she was 'resolved, in the midst and heat of the battle, to live or die amongst you all, to lay down my life for my God and for my kingdom and for my people, my honour, and my blood, even in the dust'. She also famously drew attention to the fact that she had 'the body of a weak and feeble woman', but that she had 'the heart and stomach of a king' and, moreover, for patriotic emphasis 'a king of England too'. Here she may well have been referring to her father Henry VIII, thus affirming her royal lineage and that 'she is her father's daughter'. Art historians have made the case that the Darnley Portrait (page 49) was deliberately conceived to accentuate the physical similarities between Henry and Elizabeth. Henry was invariably portrayed as an exemplar of Renaissance masculinity and virility; copies of Holbein's now-lost 'Whitehall' portrait show a commanding full-length pose and prominent over-sized codpiece. In the Armada Portrait, Elizabeth's 'weak and feeble' body is concealed and protected by the exaggerated magnificence and commanding scale of her dress, giving the queen the appearance, in outline at least, of broad shoulders to rival Henry's powerful physique. This may in part symbolise the medieval idea of the 'king's two bodies' – the spiritual or divine body, wherein lies royal power, which is separate from the innate frailty of the physical body (especially poignant in reference to a queen). But it may also symbolise the associated idea of the 'body politic'. In the Tilbury speech, Elizabeth expresses 'foul scorn that Parma or Spain, or any prince of Europe should dare to invade the borders of my realm'. As the Virgin Queen, strong and impenetrable, Elizabeth can be said to personify the inviolability of the nation state. Undoubtedly the relationship between the Armada Portrait and the substance of the queen's speech would be made all the more powerful if she had worn at Tilbury the same dress as that represented in the painting.

Finally, the contrasting personas of the vulnerable woman and the powerful queen, which Elizabeth evoked to such dramatic effect at Tilbury, were clearly meant to rouse her *male* audience into defending the realm as an act of patriotism and chivalry. Two later images of Elizabeth, the Ditchley (page 68) and Rainbow (page 70) Portraits, are of interest in this regard. Both are associated with actual court masques. In these representations, in parallel with poetry and pageantry, the aging queen is transformed into an object of quasi-religious reverence. In the Ditchley Portrait at the National

Portrait Gallery, she is shown standing on – and thus in
command of – the world (her feet are positioned on Ditchley,
the Oxfordshire home of her retired Champion, Sir Henry
Lee, who probably commissioned the portrait). She is placed
between scenes of storm and calm, the inscription to the right
suggesting that Elizabeth is the Sun, thus the source of daylight
and the clement weather shown to the left. In the Armada
Portrait, the queen's elaborate ruff and the pearls in her hair
form a radiant circle around her face, which in turn implies
that the queen is benevolently radiating light over the world.
This analogy is developed further in the Rainbow Portrait at
Hatfield House created in the last years of her reign. The queen,
resplendent in a masque costume, holds a rainbow in her right
hand, above which is an inscription *non sine sol iris* ('no rainbow
without the Sun').

A specific event, the momentous Armada of 1588,
inspired the Armada Portrait, but more than that, it embraces
issues of monarchy, dynasty, nation and empire in the early

NON SINE SOLE
IRIS.

modern period. Ultimately, as a work of art, it was designed to be a spectacle of female power and majesty, carefully calibrated to inspire awe and wonder in the viewer. In many respects, the portrait still fulfils its original intention. ❀

◄ *Queen Elizabeth I, 'The Rainbow Portrait', c. 1600*
Unknown artist, c. 1600, oil on panel

This is the last major portrait of Elizabeth completed in her lifetime and it is imbued with highly complex symbolism. A jewelled serpent, an emblem of wisdom, writhes on her left sleeve, while a crescent moon surmounts the crown that forms part of an elaborate and richly ornamented headdress. The queen's cloak is lined with vivid orange silk and profusely embroidered with eyes and ears, implying, of course, that the monarch could know everything because her loyal agents were everywhere.

The conservation of the Armada Portrait at Greenwich

To display the Armada Portrait at the Queen's House in Greenwich, and ensure its survival for future generations, the National Maritime Museum undertook a major conservation project. Elizabeth Hamilton-Eddy, the Museum's Senior Paintings Conservator, thoroughly assessed the portrait and recommended a course of action. She had worked on the painting twice before when it was lent to the Museum for temporary exhibitions on the Spanish Armada in 1988 and on Elizabeth I in 2003. However, the purchase of the portrait allowed an opportunity to investigate its construction, the techniques employed by the unknown artist, and the extent of historic damage and the nature of subsequent repairs far more rigorously than before.

The first task of the complex project was to clean the portrait by removing several layers of old, discoloured varnish, which included one of toned varnish that a restorer had probably applied to give the painting an 'antique' look. This process began with a series of tiny cleaning tests to establish the most suitable solvent, or solvent mix, for this delicate task. Once the varnish and obvious later overpainting were gone,

work could begin on consolidating the surface by securing
any raised or fragile areas of paint and addressing a crude
earlier repair to the queen's chin, which appeared even more
disfiguring without the varnish. As hidden details and old
damages were uncovered, careful judgements were made by
Hamilton-Eddy in consultation with colleagues throughout
this crucial stage. A key consideration was how to treat the two
seascapes. Earlier x-ray photography, plus a new, more advanced
and comprehensive method known as macro XRF scanning,
revealed that beneath the seascapes were painted panels similar
in design to those in the Woburn version. But the results of

chemical analysis revealed that the visible paint layer contained an early form of Prussian blue, meaning the scenes with late-seventeenth-century-style ships had been painted at some point relatively soon after the introduction of the new pigment in 1710. Accepting that these 300-year-old scenes were now an integral part of the Greenwich Armada Portrait, the decision was made, on sound historic and conservation grounds, to conserve them in line with the rest of the painting.

When the first stage was complete, a new layer of synthetic varnish was applied. This served two purposes: it saturated the colours of the original paint, bringing back the vibrancy of the Tudor portrait; and it created a barrier between the original layers and the painstaking retouching of what had been lost over time. Everything added to restore the appearance of the portrait was, therefore, entirely removable, limited to areas of historic loss, and stable, meaning it would not discolour over time. A final layer of varnish meant that work to the portrait itself was complete: conservation was a six-month-long effort. The painting was then placed in a microclimate frame and glazed with low-reflect glass. This ensured that the five fragile panels on which the portrait is painted would be less susceptible to damage from any movement caused by changes in temperature and humidity, and that the painted surface was protected from dust and other pollutants. The results of Hamilton-Eddy's expertly executed conservation project are plain to see: the Armada Portrait has been rejuvenated and returned to majestic magnificence. ❀

▲ Detail showing the difference in colour before and after conservation work on the Armada Portrait at Greenwich

Index

Sources and further reading

Helen Castor, *Elizabeth I: a Study in Insecurity* (London: Penguin, 2018).

James Davey, ed., *Tudor and Stuart Seafarers: the Emergence of a Maritime Nation, 1485–1714* (London: Adlard Coles, 2018).

M.J. Rodríguez-Salgado, ed., *Armada, 1588–1988* (London: Penguin, 1988).

David Scott, *Leviathan: the Rise of Britain as a World Power* (London: Harper Press, 2013).

Kevin Sharpe, *Selling the Tudor Monarchy: Authority and Image in Sixteenth-Century England* (London: Yale University Press, 2009).

Roy Strong, *The Elizabethan Image: an Introduction to English Portraiture, 1558 to 1603* (London: Yale University Press, 2019).

Roy Strong, *Gloriana: the Portraits of Elizabeth I* (London: Thames & Hudson, 1987).